Ebby Thatcher
Bill Wilson

The Prehistory of Alcoholics Anonymous

History of Recovery

Transcribed from Historic Sound Recordings

DEDICATION

This book and the restored audio recordings it was transcribed from is dedicated to everyone who enjoys learning about the history of Alcoholics Anonymous from recordings of people who were around and were part of the beginnings of Alcoholics Anonymous.

TABLE OF CONTENTS

CHAPTER ONE EBBY ST. LOUIS PART 1

This is Ebby speaking from Saint Louis the 20th Anniversary Convention of AA. I am very happy to be here. I consider myself fortunate in being able to make the trip from Dallas, Texas, where I am now living. It's good to see Bill again. I haven't seen much of him in the last couple of years; although he did make the trip to Fort Worth at the Texas State Convention, a year ago this past June.

As a good many people know, I attended school in Manchester, Vermont, with Bill Wilson, in 1912. I was born in Albany, NY and attended the Albany Academy in that city, and I summered in Manchester. And, in 1911 and 1912 I formed a great friendship with the son of the minister in the Congregational Church in that town. This boy's name was Roger Perkins, and I believe as I look back that he had a great deal to do with giving me many fine ideas about life he was a splendid chap. He joined the naval aviation in World War One and was killed, in Pensacola Florida, flying. Bill and I. also were, very close friends. During that year in school, and we spent a good many hours talking together. I returned to my school in Albany, but I never finished out.

I believe it was in 1914 sometime in the winter, February January, somewhere along there; I walked into the hotel tonight in Albany and ordered myself a glass of beer. Very probably I had a sip of wine or something at home prior to that, at a dinner party, but this was the first occasion of actually, going in and buying a drink. And, I know that that glass of beer tasted very wonderful to me.

And, I tried it again not too long afterwards. And, the drinking grew from then on, times when I could handle it and times when I could not; I was an in and outer. Right then, decidedly showing signs of alcoholism from the beginning.

As time went on of course, I didn't see much of Bill because he lived in New York and Brooklyn. I live in Albany, although we did see each other on occasions and in Manchester during the summer time. I didn't seem much of Bill until about 1927 and '28. When Bill was in the investment business, and so was I. I was in the Albany office working for a New York firm. Bill appeared upon the scene in Albany one Saturday, and found me downtown and I immediately joined him. And, we took on some drinks, for the first time that ever had a drink together.

And, I was playing around with a bunch of flyers in Albany and they were barnstorming. We are in the airport, which was rather new. And, I took Bill out to a party that night at one of the apartments where some of these lads gathered and girls. And somebody either Bill or I, I got the brilliant idea (Bill was on his way to Vermont), that we charter a plane to, fly out.

So I promoted the idea. I was all for it and I got a chap named Ted Burke and I believe that when we left Ted he didn't think we were going through it, but, I remember I took Bill to a hotel, put him up and I went out and drank all night.

I went down and got Bill next morning and we went over and got Ted out of bed; a bit disgruntled and out to the airport and we found Vermont. They said it was clear weather up there. The post of the airstrip is about the size of postage stamp. It's kind of a tough deal for a pilot to fly two drunks up there. But the trip was uneventful, except that most of Manchester gathered the airport and we staggered out of the plane upon arrival, which wasn't too good.

But, conditions of course got worse with both of us in the drinking line. But I, after my father's death, I went to live in Manchester; Well, this was in 1932; I lived at an Inn, out there and then I went and opened the house which my father had bought, a few years previous. And I lived in that house all alone. This was in 1934 in the spring. And I was drinking pretty hard and during the course of that drinking up to about August I had been in the toils of the law twice; fined both of those times for intoxication.

It was sometime in July or August, I have forgotten which, but two old friends came to see me, they dropped down at the house one afternoon. Now these chaps were not what I would really call alcoholic, but they had been heavy drinkers. Well, they sacked me and just chewed the Rag awhile and kind of fussed around. And then they told me that they joined an organization called the Oxford Group. That they had found a great deal of spiritual value in it; that it helped them iron out their lives, and they came right out with the statement, "Why don't you try turning your life over to God, as you understand him?" which was the principle, one of the principles of how the Oxford Group operated.

And the more they talked the more, I was impressed. (It) struck me that, this was a simple religion or religious ideas rather that I had had with childlike faith as a young chap, as a very small boy. Of which, of course, I had lost, perhaps not lost but perhaps dormant. Well, they left me a book. I have forgotten the name of that book right now, but it was written by a chap who is associated with the Oxford Group and there was a lot of very good common sense. It dealt with the business man and the drinking and the roaring 20s, and how he had found something to live by and to clean up his life. (probably I WAS A PAGAN by V.C. Kitchen) And I was impressed with the whole thing, but like so many of us, I still wanted to fool with a bottle.

But, I made a deal with a painter. I'd been trying to paint the House alone and I just gave it up. I couldn't get up the ladder, half the time, and so I gave it up, but I made a deal with the painter and he sent a man around with some equipment.

So we could string planks between two ladders to serve as a scaffold. And I really sobered up and finished that house, with this chap. But as soon as I was done; you know the old monotony of life and nothing to look forward to, so I went back to drinking, with the result that my neighbors complained and I was again hauled in front of the law.

I forgot to mention that there had been a third chap come to see me, whom I had not known prior to this, and his name is Rowland. The other two chaps were Cebra and Shep. Well, at the time when I was hauled in front of the judge at the County seat. Rowland appeared and I was released in his custody.

Uh, Rowland had been abroad in Switzerland and had taken a course under (Dr Carl) Jung, the Swiss psychiatrist and then, consequently affiliated with this Oxford Group. Well, I spent a few days back in in the house. Rowland drove me back up there. It was a Monday morning. And there's one thing that I would like to mention here. No, I I'm ahead of myself. I was first taking down on Friday... the judge said you come back here for further hearing on Monday. It was then that I was taken back to the house.

And I went down cellar because I knew I had four or five bottles of ale left and they were alright cool and I was shaking pretty badly. And I started to open one of these bottles and still small voice says "No, that's not cricket." You can... and then this other voice says "Well this is nonsense. You won't be able to get anymore liquor in town, you've got Saturday and Sunday and you can nurse that ale along and you're not going to be drunk. The judge said, come back sober, but he didn't say anything about taking a drink." But I just couldn't take that. I put the thing down and walk upstairs and come down the cellar again. So finally I put the ale under my arm and took them over and gave them to the man next door.

Come out after doing that, I felt a great release. Well, Rowland and I were closely associated for a long time then and I went to spend some time with him. He lived about 15 miles below Manchester in Vermont. And we had some people up and we went out and they made me start in speaking right away. We took a trip through Vermont. We spoke five times in one weekend; at a couple of churches, a junior college, and a couple of private gatherings, in people's homes. Then Rowland drove me to New York and I lived with Shep for a while in his apartment, on East 57th street.

And then I went to live in the mission operated by Calvary Episcopal Church. I might say Calvary Episcopal Church was at that time considered the headquarters of the Oxford Group in America. Not the church itself, but the parish house rather. Well, I was one of the twelve of the brotherhood or so called who operated the mission and as I went around, of course I saw a great deal of my old friends in New York and I learned that Bill had been hitting the bottle pretty heavily. And so much so that he lost most of his connections in Wall Street, and was in bad all around town, same as I had been in Albany in my hometown.

Well, I thought the thing over, and I determined to go see Bill, because of our old friendship. Because I saw that if Bill takes a hold of this thing; well he'll go far on it. And I really felt when I went over there that he would either go for it lock, stock and barrel, or he would reject it entirely. I didn't think there would be any half way measure. And you know, most of you know that story. Of course it's been. It's in the big book. And where I saw Bill, had a talk with him, had a little dinner first, Lois. I know the girl who was there as I was a friend of theirs as later we all adjourned upstairs and, oh, I talked I guess till maybe one o'clock. I remember some things, of course, some details of that talk that perhaps Bill does not remember.

For instance, when I left Bill walked to the subway with me and put his arms around my shoulder. He said "I don't know what you got Ebby but you got something that I want. Bill didn't stop drinking right away the same as I didn't, but he evidently was thinking about it. Because he appeared at the mission a few nights later visibly intoxicated, and with a sailor in tow that he picked up somewhere. Bill was sitting there when the various boys were giving testimony all of sudden; Bill got up, strode up to the platform, and started to speak. Most people don't know this, but the Superintendent came over and said we should get him down, I said, let him speak. He's got something on his mind let him get it off his chest. And he did, he talked right there? I don't think most people know this particular incident.

Later on, as Bill told you I followed up in Towns Hospital and I saw a great deal of him when he first came out. Kind of kept close tabs on him; and as time went on we were very close. I lived in the mission for a year, at the end of this year I joined Bill and Lois at their invitation and lived with them for another year. At which time I returned to Albany as I felt that is the place where I caused most of my trouble through drinking. And I felt that most of my restitution should be done back there.

CHAPTER TWO EBBY ST. LOUIS PART 2

Perhaps I have left out some of the things that these men, connected with the Oxford Group had taught me. It is hard to go back twenty twenty-one years and remember these things exactly. But the Oxford Group was based on a return to First Century Christian Fellowship. (Like very early Christianity, the Oxford Group had no leadership hierarchy and didn't own buildings.)

And, right now I am reminded that the Reverend Sam Shoemaker. Who is nominal head of the Oxford Group in this country, and who taught me so much, is present at this convention in Saint Louis. And I had the pleasure of having a couple of short chats with him and last night walked home from a convention with him.

The Oxford Group had four so called principles, somewhat similar to the 12 steps of Alcoholics Anonymous. From which four principles I think that the 12 steps were built on. These were absolute honesty, absolute love, absolute unselfishness and absolute purity. Of course, these were, as these chaps told me. These were broken down into workable everyday living. The Oxford Group advocated the principle of morning meditation or as they called it quiet time when you tried to release yourself. Wipe out self and see if you couldn't get in tune with God, as you understood Him, and see if you couldn't get some guidance for the day, and to hold yourself flexible not make any set plans, wherein it is possible to do so, and try to meet each situation as it came up and meet it believing that it was God's will that these events that came up should transpire as they do. In other words, to accept what came each day. And as you know, in A.A. it's done on a twenty four hour basis. Just take things as they come each day.

Since I've been in in Texas I have seen more and more of the daily contract that these chaps make with God each morning. God, keep me from taking a drink today. You can easily see how this sprang from the teachings of the Oxford Group. It was very inclusive. The indoctrination was very thorough. They had a great many meetings similar to A.A. Meetings today run along the same sort of procedure. And they also had a great many so called team meetings; where people would express their thoughts freely and people would take notes. And, it was really good; sharing your life and your troubles and your mistakes and your errors, and you're imposing self into everything with other people. And it was a great catharsis. It helped immeasurably. It helped me, I know.

But my return to Albany I perhaps began to fall back into my old ways of living. At first they had a small nucleus of people in the city that were trying to get an Oxford Group going, but there were not many, and they were not Alcoholics. Although I had calls at several times to go out and see some of my old drinking buddies.

One chap and his wife in particular; I knew nothing about the wife's drinking, but when I went out to talk to them, well, he never actually got ahold of it very well, but she sobered up, and as far as I know she had little if any trouble since that time. She became very much interested in the Oxford Group. In fact, here in the convention last night I got a bit of word over from some man who knew them and he said that she was doing very well and I'm happy to hear this, but the Oxford Group did not flourish as such in Albany.

It was 1936 when I returned to Albany and I got a job in the fall of 1936 in the Ford Motor Company in Green Island, which is about twelve miles north of Albany. And I worked at that job for nearly six months. I had a time when I was working on the night shift to make trips to New York and I kept in touch with Bill and the boys down there and they were beginning to the form plans for writing a book; Alcoholics Anonymous, the big book and one of these trips down there in April, the latter of part of April 1937. After two years and seven months of complete sobriety. I slipped one night. And of course, I immediately got in touch with some people.

I was staying at the Lexington Hotel and the next morning there were over bright and early and took me over to Bills. Bill was going away and over the weekend, I believe, and I was there in the house alone, and of course I had started this vicious circle again and I kept on almost all of that week returning to Albany and returning to my job the following Monday morning, Ford Motor Company. And I was still pretty shaky. I punched my card and the general Superintendent came along and he says "Well, where were you all last week?" I said that I was sick. That's my story and I'm going to stick to it. And he smiled and said "Alright go on out there and go to work."

I was working in the Spring Division as an Inspector. But when I got down there, and my immediate boss had pretty much of a grouch on, and he said "Have we got a job for you today. He said "The cranes broken down on the yard; we've go to unload a car of steel." So he said "Get going." Well, I went out there and at the end of about two hours I couldn't open my hands. I was unloading these bundles of strip steel. One man would pass them to me, and the two of us would take them over and pile them up. I stuck it out all day but at the end of that day I was pretty much all in and I drove home with a man who took me to work on the day shift.

I was on the day shift that time. And he said, "I have been trying to borrow some money," he said, "around the place," he said, "Because I know that you need a drink" he said "that I couldn't get a cent," he said, "everybody's broke-Monday morning." I said "That's alright, I've got it." So we went to a saloon and that was the last Mister

Ford ever saw me. A few days later, the man came round and got the badge and gave me the check; money that was coming to me.

Well, there's no use going into details; when it's been bad, and it's been good; off and on all these years. I went through Philadelphia in the spring of 1941. I've been in a place in New Jersey, which is a religious place for Alcoholics. And well, they make you work pretty hard. We were out all that winter, tearing up an old track, an old railroad track, and getting the ties and we were using them as firewood we laid in quite a supply of that. It was good rugged work 'cause it was cold in that railroad cut. But, I went to Philadelphia and I guess I drove up with someone. Got there about 10:00 o'clock in the morning and I was drinking by 12. I couldn't stand the city after the country or something like that; at least that was the excuse.

And I got in a room and I drank myself out of the room and I was in the park, Fairmount Park sitting around. And finally I had recourse to call on A.A., and they took me to Philadelphia General where I spent four or five days in the psycho ward. And then, I went down some people who had connections with this place in New Jersey where I had been and I got a job with them. They were an association very much similar to the Salvation Army only it was just a local organization and I worked on that truck, picking up stuff, newspapers, furniture, everything, oh, I think about six weeks. Then I made a shift to a hospital; worked as a Porter for three months. In the meantime, I had made an application to the United States Navy Department, as an Inspector. And it was getting along to the fall of 1941 then. And the first reports from my application was that I was turned down, but after Pearl Harbor, they sent me another notice that I was satisfactory so, I worked, I went right from the hospital job to job as inspector with the Navy. This job I held for about 16 months. I was sober all this time. But after we had the contract licked and this plant, I was stationed in a private plant, I again lost interest. And I had no way of getting out of the Navy so I again took the course of the bottle.

And they were awfully nice to me. They sent a couple of guys over to see me and they said take two or three days off and have some fun because you deserve it. We know your record. You didn't take a drink on the job and your work is satisfactory all the way through. But I just couldn't snap out of it. Then I was too far gone and I just kept on drinking finally they gave me released without prejudice; reason ill health.

Well, I batted around Philadelphia sobering up, and then, getting drunk again. I served as a steward of the A.A. Club at South 36th St in Philadelphia, Two or three occasions. Jobs with Westinghouse, job with an Army like outside contractor who was crating trucks for overseas shipment; I really had a good job there, and several other jobs. Years went on and I finally returned in New York in 1945. And since then, after the time I left New York in September 1953 for Dallas. It was in and out all the time sober, eight months, drunk a couple months, sober six months, drinking again. Of course I do not want anybody to get the impression I've been drunk all the time, because that's not so. In the last twenty years if you count up the months of sobriety I can total them up to fourteen years easily. And sometimes people forget that.

I have had a little trouble since I've been in Dallas. I had about five or six days of drinking. Well, I've also had twenty one and a half months or so of clear sobriety. I have been closely associated with the suburban group, of Dallas, and I have found a great deal of help from the members and the spirit which pervades that group.

I thought I would like to go back. For a moment to the spiritual part of the AA program which perhaps sprang from the teachings of the Oxford Group, from the members, from some very wonderful people in this world who are not Alcoholics have all had a hand in it. But I recall that Rowland who spent a year in Switzerland with (Doctor Carl) Jung told me that; I cannot quote this exactly after so many years, but the gist of it was that (Doctor Carl) Jung had told him that while he, (Doctor Carl) Jung could take Rowland apart, and show him these things. He doubted if he would ever have any complete success with his drinking; with an alcoholic problem until he had a spiritual experience. Until his idea of God, his belief in God had become a part of him. And that would come from within. So (Doctor Carl) Jung himself knew that without the spiritual side there was very little hope for most Alcoholics.

I believe, I believe this fairly; because we cannot do anything alone; we try we're pigheaded we're stubborn. I know that in my case. It has been my stumbling block; trying to take the reins away from God; when I knew and felt that only He could lead me. When I returned to Albany, after two years of complete sobriety, I felt, in my heart, I guess it has been creeping in that I've been a good little boy now and I like the boy who wanted a present from Santa Claus Christmas. I felt that one or two things that I desired and wished all my life should be granted me. Well, evidently it was not to be. And it is taking me years and years and years to release these things.

I do believe that since coming to Texas, I have sort of left behind. I think that the night I took the plane from LaGuardia Airport. I left behind a couple of these things which I had tried to, to shake off in New York, but have never been able to. Things I thought were coming to me, or justly due. On which, and the plan of things were not met. And I never could, although I repeated the serenity prayer time and time again and never gotten really inside of me. I never could lose these things but I have been feeling a release from them since I've been out here.

And it didn't happen all at once, it was gradual. But it was the same kind of release that I felt that day that I didn't take the ale when I was back in Vermont. And I do hope. And believe it with the help of God and my daily trying to keep in touch with Him. And keeping in contact with all AA's I do believe with all His help I will be able to lick this alcoholic problem.

CHAPTER THREE BILL WILSON PART 1

Good morning dear people. I would like to renew the thanks that Lois gave for the privilege of being with this magnificent crowd. We have heard unsurpassed talks on every aspect of that benign, that providential synthesis which is our society. We have seen and felt and heard expressions of its spiritual essence. Of it's moral substance. We are reminded that our malady was lack of a life in the spirit; lack of morality, but lest we get too guilty. We are also happily reminded that this is also a bodily disease.

You know, I recently went to Sister Ignatia's funeral, and in a very real sense it was a time not for mourning, but of rejoicing. That God, had been so good to us all, and there, as the minds eye turns back to those early days; we can see Doctor Bob, representing Medicine and A.A. and Sister Ignatia, all the best in religion. Again, it was the

Divine Synthesis of which this group, in my belief are these special inheritors.

In the middle of the 19th century, a new means of communication, burst upon the world. To set in motion a train of events of consequences, that even now cannot be reckoned. This was the telegraph. It is a matter of great significance, and meaning at least to us that the first words, sent over the first wire between Washington and Baltimore were these, and they apparently characterize the inventor. The words were "What hath God wrought."

So today, over a retrospect of thirty years we are watching building of a new means of communication characterized not by material things, but a new way of speaking the language of the heart, one to another. And this language is a varied language, and we have participated in one of its magnificent variations in this meeting having in it these components of Science and of the Spirit; the only synthesis of any great promise to the world of our time.

In a sense I suppose our beginnings are infinite ages old, because there has never been any age in which the impulse to reach for a Higher Power was absent since man became conscious.

Then came the Carpenter, and of course, we are in His tradition, and teaching, but I would like to pinpoint, in terms of people, who the personal candle bearers were in the beginning, and I am happy to say, especially so, since we have heard so much good natured, and perhaps not so good natured derogation of psychiatrists, that this man, happened to be a psychiatrist. And in the view, many of whom I am one, one of the great figures, of our generation, I speak of Carl Jung. One of the three, founders of the modern art of depth psychology. He was distinguished from the other founders, in that he felt, and I am sure, knew, in his inner heart that man was something more, than a modicum of intelligence often ill used; he was something more than a bundle of instinct, something more than two dollars worth of chemicals. I am sure of this because I know people who have been in contact, and one of my chief regrets is that a correspondence that we had begun before his death had not been started years earlier.

So vision, if you will a prominent American businessman, who I shall call Rowland. Rowland was a typical case. He had exhausted every resource that he knew, so he came to Carl Jung, and they spent a year together. And Rowland became convinced that now so many of the hidden springs of his strange compulsions and motivations stood revealed that he would drink no more. Leaving the doctor, he was drunk within a month. To him, this was a ghastly experience. This was the end, and he came back to Doctor Carl, and said, "Carl, you were my court of last resort. Is there anything else?

And this very kind old gentleman said Rowland "I thought that you might have been one of those rare cases in which my art might help you to sobriety and better things, but now I know your case is that of such gravity, and complication that my art will not unravel it." And the patient took another dive toward deflation at depth; the basis on which our whole recovery rests. He hit bottom.

But he persisted "Doctor is there no other recourse for me?" And the dear old gentleman said, "Rowland, yes, there may be, but I must be frank with you it doesn't happen too often. I speak to you, of a conversion experience." Oh but Ah said Rowland "I used to be a vestryman in the church; my faith has still not left me." "But this hasn't worked,"

Jung said "I am talking about something that goes beyond faith; I am talking about a transforming experience, in which the recipient, as a gift, appears to undergo a motivation, change, that cannot be accounted for by simple faith, by environment, by motivation, by association. These profound changes seem to transcend, the sum of all of the ordinary resources that can be brought to bear."

Now, he said, "Among alcoholics as among other men of all time. These profoundly transforming experiences have occurred here and there, we cannot tell to whom or when the Lightning of Providence will flash. So I suggest that you immerse yourself, in a religious atmosphere; remembering your personal helplessness, and pray for God's will."

So that is a word picture. Of the colloquy that took place between these two men, about 1932. And this great and humble man had placed the first candle which was to illuminate the table at which we sup.

Rowland associated himself with the Oxford groups then in Europe, and practiced their principles, none of which was new. They had an emphasis. There was the idea of one person talking to the next. You know the rest of it. Our basics were abstracted from it. And unaccountably Rowland seem to be released. He hadn't been educated out of drinking; he had been released from it.

Then he came to America where he fell under the spell of Doctor Sam Shoemaker, one of the founders of the Oxford Group that old time. And Sam was then also rector at an Episcopal church that stood at 23rd Street in New York. And in the Oxford Groups there were a handful of drunks who had been released; most of them rather temporarily but genuine release nevertheless by this sort of practice and attitude.

And Rowland bethought himself of an old school friend of mine. This school friend is the one so affectionately known to us as Ebby (Thatcher). Now I'll pause here, having illustrated to you this stream of influence beginning with (Doctor Carl)

Jung, to the O G (Oxford Groups), to (Rowland) Hazard.

Now let's come down the on the other tack, and see what happened at the confluence.

CHAPTER FOUR BILL WILSON PART 2

I'd gone the route the story is old you, you've read it; I've told you a thousand times the story of my drinking. So I shall quickly bring myself to that day in 1934 midsummer; when another physician was speaking dear old Doctor Silkworth, who certainly will be known in our annals as a medical saint for so long as A.A. shall last.

Someone once wrote a Grapevine piece about him. And the title was this The Little Doctor Who Loved Drunks, and from the point of view of the rationalist and the scientific man, the little doctor was a nobody, even crank with odd ideas. He said; that sure there is a lunatic compulsion to drink, certainly true enough. No doubt it may have psychological causes, trauma and use etc. but he said, I think that there is a big moral question. And he also said, I believe, that there is something wrong with the body and the metabolism of alcoholics. For short, not knowing what it is I use a widely understood term called allergy.

So this adds up to a compulsion that condemns the victim to drink against his will and interest until the destruction is complete. And this is joined to a physical condition that ensures his lunacy and finally his demise.

On this hot summer night, this dear little man who up to then had worked in drying out joints, finally Towns Hospital where I used to go, with perhaps twenty-five thousand drunks, occasional successes here and there. He worked on a pittance. He boarded in the place. He had a room upstairs.

So, as gently as he could, he told Lois what the score was. Just like (Doctor Carl) Jung speaking to Rowland, he said. "When Bill came here, he clearly wanted so desperately to stop that I thought he might be one of the few but I'm afraid that I must say that he isn't. He's beginning to be deteriorating I'm afraid if he would remain sane or even live long that he will have to be committed.

So this is the sentence that Science, in the persons of Doctor Jung and Doctor Silkworth passed upon me and upon all of us and both these truly great men, great human beings have had the courage to say what they believe.

Well, meanwhile, my friend Ebby, had got into such a state that he was about to be committed for lunacy at a state institution in Vermont where the family is from. The town fathers had wearied of Ebby (Audience Laughter). For the town fathers, this was it. So they gathered up Ebby, hailed him before the judge down at Bennington, and just as he was about to be routed to the hoosegow at Brattleboro (Vermont), there appeared (Rowland) Hazard along with a couple of other drunks from the Oxford Group.

And they took Ebby into tow and they got him sort of indoctrinated on the desirability of honesty, restitution, helping other people, prayer and so forth. They brought him down to New York.

Well, just after leaving the hospital. I had stayed sober for a month or two out of sheer fear, constant vigilance, and then I was in the toils again. So about the time, Ebby in New York, and was parked because he was penniless in Calvary Mission. I'm sitting at the kitchen table. Lois is working in that Department store. I had a communication a kind of a language of the heart with the delicatessen up there which supplied me with gin on credit.

And I sat drinking and the telephone rang. And now I knew that this was it. Something told me so and Science had driven in the last spike I was nailed down this day. So the telephone rang and here is Ebby. I thought he had gone to the booby hatch. I said, "Come on over. We'll talk about the good old days." Ah. What a very significant line-The Good Old Days. Today was unbearable, and there would be no future so we would talk.

He appeared in the doorway. At once I sense something in indefinably different about him. He came in. He sat at this kitchen table in the basement, on it I had a big pitcher full of gin, with a little pineapple juice splash then so as to suggest cocktails instead of the straight stuff when Lois got home from the store. So I set out the tumbler for him and started to pour.

He said "No thanks" What? No Thanks? "Well, what's got into you Ebby. Not drinking?" Well, he says "I'm not drinking today." Well, I said "Come, Let's have it what's happened?" Well, he looked at me and he said "I've got religion." Well, if I'd been deflated by the scientist, this really let me down to the middle of the art, because I had had a wonderful scientific education too. Just like our last speaker, I knew better. Well, one must be polite, so I said to Ebby "What brand is it?"

(Audience Laughter) And he said I wouldn't exactly call it a brand, and then being very careful to avoid the aggressive evangelism of the Oxford Group. He merely told me his story, how it he and (Rowland) Hazard, come to New York and (he) had felt unaccountably released from this desire to drink. Well, this release was a new one I always was talking about the water wagon.

So, his story carried great conviction to me; over this identification, no doubt at great depth. Over which, simple ideas could be pitched in. Instead of having to use the corkscrew of the psychiatrist from the top, he was able to go right straight through. He hadn't presented me with a single new idea though. But I will say that after that conversation I could never be the same man again. And so without pressuring me at all, he took his leave, said "I'll see you later."

In no waking hour in the days that followed could the vision of Ebby speaking across that table leave me. And of course I felt trapped. I said, but if I only could go along with it. Honesty, yes, you could make a try, helping other people dandy. You know I'm public spirited, etc. But the God bit, no, and this had it, really, although he had played it down, appeared to be the crux of it.

So finally, one morning after Lois had gone and I got partly tanked up. I said I've got to get a clear look at this thing. So I arrived up at Towns Hospital, half stewed. Doctor Silkworth looked at me sadly. And I brandished the bottle and yelled "Doc, This time I got something." And the old man said, "I'm afraid you have you better get upstairs and go to bed."

Well, you know the rest of the story. I fussed around New York with drunks. The experience had a certain paranoid component. I was prone to grandiosity. I think I announced during first six months. I was going to fix all the drunks in the world, which was a long departure from experience. Ego came back. There wasn't a damn one got fixed until I arrived in Akron.

And here was dear Doctor Bob. And so I said, "I'm going to quit preaching." "I'm going to quit demanding that these people have an experience like mine indeed." And this was another cornerstone. If I am to stay, sober myself, for I had been disconcerted by the failure of a business deal. I need this other alcoholic; drunk or sober worse than he could ever need me. So we struck that mutuality. I got off of my pedestal, it clicked soon after there was a third, and in Akron, Bob with Sister Ignatia.

Again, in this benign synthesis, medicine, religion and her own experience launched the set of transformations running through five thousand drunks at Akron in Bob's lifetime, and with Ignatia and coworkers in the area to another ten thousand up to the time of her death.

Such is our debt, to medicine; such is our debt, to Christian teaching; such my friends, is our debt to the Everlasting and Eternal God. (Audience Applause)

CHAPTER FIVE EBBY SAN JOSE PART 1

Thank you, yes, I'm sold on San Francisco. You can say that. I had two charming ladies take me on a tour today, and they certainly did a fine job. I saw everything I wanted to see in a short time. I went to the Cliff House and saw the Embarcadero, Fisherman's Wharf from the top of the mark.

And it's nice to be here. I've been asked to go over the early ground of A.A., and to do so, I'm going to give you some of my background as a young man. I was born and raised in Albany, NY. As some of you know (Albany) is the capital of state. And my father and mother had always had, rented a summer cottage in Manchester, Vermont, which is only sixty miles away. I know it's a short trip up there by train and later on my automobile. Although I remember the first time that we made it, the car that we had built ourselves in our foundry machine shop. It took three days and then they wound up on a hill four miles south of the village. It broke down for third or fourth time. They had to be hauled in by a team of horses. I can see the local constable saying get a horse, get a horse like a clear vision I can still see my father and my older brother coming in.

And it was there and I met Bill Wilson; in Manchester, Vermont. I went to school in Albany, but I formed a great friendship with the minister's son and he went to the local school out there, the high school. He persuaded me and I in turn sold a bill of goods to my family to stay up there a winter and go to school up there.

I had met Bill casually before, but I got to know him very well at winter and we became good friends. That's where our friendship started, and of course then, Lois was a Burnham, who had a summer cottage and directly across from ours on the Main Street of town, and I knew her from childhood in fact she can remember because she's a little older than me. She can remember me when I was in the baby carriage. And so that takes us up to the time that I knew Bill Wilson.

In my last year in school, which turned out to be in my last year because I got drinking; (I) was expelled. I wasn't in fact expelled but the principle at school wrote my father a letter that they did not think they could do anything more for me, which is practically the same so I just didn't show up that fall and my father put me to work in his iron foundry.

My drinking ran somewhat regular. I would hold it down to Saturday nights although I'd get drunk. I never could tell what I was going to do. I might drink some of the older men under the table and I might get drunker than a hoot owl on three or four drinks and raise the devil and have a hard time, but I generally managed to keep it on Saturday night.

I knew as a young man, I think, that when Bill and I went to school we talked the situation over because the condition was in both our families. My father drank too much, my brothers did and I could only figure that I was just the same as they were. I mean in makeup. Temperamental makeup and I'd probably go the same way. But one time in Albany I walked into the bar room in the hotel one night and I ordered a glass of beer, and that is the finest glass of beer I ever tasted. And I said, "This is for me." Just that one beer, just that little warm feeling it gave you.

And I used it because I had no confidence as a young man in a gathering of people. I was alright with one or two of my cronies but when I got in a gathering I was lost and I found that alcohol would overcome that. I'd become more or less the life of the party and I think that's what I wanted to be. I wanted to be kingpin in everything I did probably. And yet I wasn't quite good enough, that alcohol brought me up to the point where at least I thought I was.

But it began to get pretty bad as the years went on and Saturday nights drunk are progressing to one or two nights during the week, and when the Christmas Holidays came around and the games came out and the dances, now that way. I didn't get much work done, in the foundry

I got to drinking pretty heavy. And it went from bad to worse and I have had lots of hot water, and lots of trouble. Got so I'd go on a drunk and couldn't get off it and I'm taking the first drink in the morning and that started the ball rolling right back in the bottle again.

Well let's skip a lot of the blow by blow description and get up to 1934.

I was living alone in my house in Manchester. My father and mother were both dead. And strange as it may seem, we never bought a house up there until 1923, and my mother died in 1927;

my father in 1929 and I was living at home. I was drinking to beat the devil and my brothers were all married and they had taken most of the furniture and they left some stuff for me and I lived there.

And I was trying to paint the house, alone, I had ladder. I didn't have sufficient equipment, but was too shaky to get up on that ladder. And I was making a mess of things generally. I had been arrested a couple of times for drunkenness around the town, and three times in Vermont there's a mandatory six month sentence in the state prison.

So, these fellows came along, a couple of them that I had been drinking with. Used to drink with (and had) known them for years and they collared me down to the house one day and they started talking to me about this Oxford Group they had become interested in.

And I listened because they made sense. I know that; I don't think that they were alcoholics in the sense that I am. They both drank heavily. But I think the liquor (was secondary) they were more or less power hungry, both of them, one was a New York stock broker, and he just wanted to have a world by the horns where he could run it.

But they talked a lot of sense to me and they left a book with me and they said now "You can try to run your life your own way; Down on your luck, not getting anywhere and drinking yourself to death." "Why don't you try turning your life over to God?" Well that made sense to me, and I sobered up for a few days.

I wrote my brother a note that I'd like to get some help on the house and he wrote back and said go ahead, get local painter and, see what kind of a deal you can make with him. Well this man had sent over a lot of equipment and one of his painters and the two of us got the thing done.

We took over two weeks to do it because it's a big house and a lot of work still to be done around, cutting sashes on the windows and everything. Well as soon as that house was painted I lost all interest again. There was nothing to look forward to; no goal to strive for at least that house painting was something to be done, to get accomplished. So I went right back in the bottle again. And I was apprehended by local law, third time. And I appeared before the judge down in Bennington (Vermont), the local Constable, whom I went to school with that one year took me down there. And (I) appeared before him (the Judge) and it so happened that he was the father of one of the boys that had come to see me, Cebra Graves, this was Judge Graves, his father. (muddled words roughly translated as "he questioned my sobriety" NOTE: Honorable judges do not allow the testimony of intoxicated persons.) He said, "You be back here Monday. I want you back here, sober." And this may seem a very little incident but in my life it was a big one, I really messed up.

When the boys, the lads and I, drove me back to the house; I went in there all alone. I remembered that I had three nice cold bottles of ale down cellar. And I said, well, if I drink that ale and space it along it will just sort of keep me up a little bit I won't hit the depths, and I can't possibly get drunk because I can't get anymore in town. Everybody knows about this and I'm shut off my supply. And I walked down cellar and I picked up one those bottles and I said, No wait a minute judge said come back sober yet this isn't exactly cricket. Don't take a drink, is what he meant, really. And you could get back there sober and he would never know anything about it. But it isn't exactly honest.

So I walked upstairs again and I got up there and heard the bells; devils saying go down and take that ale. And I walked up and down the stairs three or four times. And finally I picked them up and put him in a carton and took him over to the man next door and said here's a present for you and believe me that was a weight was lifted off my shoulders, it really was. I felt a release from that time on.

And I know that night set down beside my bed said my prayers like I hadn't said them in years. And I said to God, I said "I really mean it; I want to quit this drinking."

Well, I stayed around the house for a couple of weeks, in October, and it began to get cold -there weren't adequate- and I didn't want to start the furnace and the hot water thing. And one of these men that had come to see me whom I didn't know- there's a third man that had come along into the picture, and he also had become interested in the Oxford Group. And he said, well, why don't you shut up the house and come down and stay with me for a few days he lived in town below about fifteen miles below south of

Manchester and he had a home there; he said "Why don't you live with me and we've got a lot of speaking to do."

Less than two weeks after I joined this thing without doing anything. I was out talking my head off it. At various places in Vermont in one week I must have talked five times at two churches, a junior college, and two town meetings. I don't know what I spoke about - running- I guess that people could sense the fact that I had found something. So that went on for awhile and we had people up from New York for something called a house party, that's what the Oxford Group called them.

And then I went down to New York and I stayed with all these lads that had come to see me for a week or two weeks. And then he made an arrangement with Calvary Episcopal Church, who ran a mission on 23rd St and 1st Avenue in what they call the gas house district used to be called that. For me to go down there; they had a

Brotherhood of Twelve Men who ran the place; supposedly on the Oxford Group line, using the principles. So I went down there and lived for a year. I sometimes I think that I shouldn't have done that. Maybe go there, but they wanted me to do it. The only reason is I think I got lazy I didn't want to get out of work too hard. I mean they let us make money and I made just enough to get by. I had a place to sleep that didn't cost me anything. Well on the other hand maybe it was meant.

And in passing I. I don't know whether many of you know much about the Oxford Group. I'm not too familiar with it but Mr. Glass tells me that he's been a member of it. I'm not sure. Sure who started it except that it was started by a man named Frank Buchman who was a member of the cloth. Somewhere in the early 30s it was 1934 when I came into the picture. And I think the great interest in it at that time perhaps was due to the Wall Street Crash of 1929.

People who had lost everything; their shirt and everything else in that crash realized that they had been paying devotion to false gods. But they were not, that they were not on the right track, and they were completely lost. And they were searching for something and they heard of it and came there. And of course, among that number were great many, alcoholics like myself.

And I was there. And I really went into the thing with spirit and tried my best to learn everything they had to teach and they were pretty thorough in the indoctrination. They had some very fine men and very wise men too. And I tried my level best to get something out of that. I think the reason that they failed, although I understand that they're still in existence out here on the West Coast under the name of Moral Rearmament. They changed the name and that name in itself was a misnomer. Because the thing started here in this country and people went over to Oxford University, in England, and in time from there they sent what they call a team to South Africa and some reporters there got a hold of it and referred to them as the group from Oxford. And that name stuck and it was called The Oxford Group, and it's no more the Oxford Group than the man in the moon.

But I tried and it was during this time that I was living and had gotten into the mission and I heard about Bill. I heard that he was drinking heavily and was not wanted in very many offices in Wall Street where he worked. That he made such a mess of himself. So I intended that maybe that I can help him and I really put some thought into it because I knew that Bill would either take it, lock, stock and barrel and go for it and he'd really put his weight behind and get in and push, or he'd reject it. And I think the reason he accepted this was because trying to get sober after so many years of drunkenness, and he was in great need at the time. It just so happened that I was the man who came along at the right time when Bill needed it with what happened to be the right medicine.

So Bill came and went to the Oxford Group meetings with me. And we did a lot of work together. Bill, from when I first saw him that night didn't sober up right away, then three or four days later he came to one of our meetings at the mission. We had meetings there every night. We had new men and we gave them beds when we could and we did have available beds.

And Bill came there drunk and even insisted on getting up on the rostrum and making a speech. And the Superintendent said "Get him down." I said, "Let him go let's see what he's got." Well he was all twisted up but he had gotten something out of my talk as we walked to the subway that night and he said, "I don't know what you got but whatever it is. I want it."

So next thing I know it was that he'd gone to Towns Hospital but he got himself three or four bottles of beer and a taxi and he drank the beer on the way up, in the taxi. And I went up and visited him there two or three times and when he got out I sort of rode herd on him, got him to come around to meetings, and pretty soon he really took a hold of the thing. And he in turn went out as you know the following summer and met Doctor Bob in Akron, and formed that great friendship that Great Fellowship that was so necessary to the founding of A.A. along with the Sister out there (Sister Ignatia) though I can't think of her name which was so necessary to the founding of A.A.

CHAPTER SIX EBBY SAN JOSE PART 2

In fact Akron claims to be the first A.A. group, of course I don't see how, because from the Oxford Group meetings there continued the meetings at Bill's house in Brooklyn, and then we went to Steinway Hall. And New York had a group that was in perfect succession all the time, but when it became Alcoholics Anonymous and springing out from the Oxford Group I can't say and I don't think Bill can or anybody. Nobody kept a diary. Nobody knew what it was all about. And you go back 27 years. It's pretty hard to remember all the tales to get things straight, the book came out about 1939, and of course that was a great incentive. And so was the article in the Saturday Evening Post, Jack Alexander.

So in the summer of 1936, I've been in New York nearly two years. I decided to go back to Albany. I lived in the mission and I moved from the mission over to Bill Wilson's house and I wasn't doing much more than laying up and Bill was good to me and I had no other place. I'd better go back to Albany my hometown where I made such a mess of things, and where I had so many amends to make. And I did. I went that summer in July or August.

I finally got a job at Ford Motor Company up in Green Island, which is eight or nine miles north of Albany. I worked for two weeks on the day shift and two weeks on the night. I used to come down (to New York) when I was working on the night shift we go through Thursday morning. (I) wasn't due back in till Sunday had come down to New York probably every third or fourth weekend. And I don't know I was getting away from attractive. I was getting away from what I had found that I guess some one thing that I wanted but God had given me and I figured that something was wrong that this little boy had been mistreated.

So I got off. I know that one of the men that works with the employees said that the last week before you went to New York that last trip you looked like piece of steel wire, because you were so tense because I knew something was going to happen. He wasn't an alcoholic himself.

I used to see a girl down there, there was no romance in it, she was just a friend and take her out at dinner. I took her out to dinner this one night and she always had a scotch highball, possibly two. That was all of it. She didn't need anymore that was enough. So she just enjoyed it, a little pick up. Well this night I ordered one, and she said "What are you going to do kick your legs out from under you. You got you got three or four months, nearly a year of sobriety, or two years of sobriety. You're going to kick it all, throw it away. I said, "One drink won't hurt me." Oh no, that night at 12:00 o'clock she finally got the taxi to let me off the Lexington Hotel, New York, and got rid of me because I was roaring drunk at that time.

And I called Bill up and he sent a couple of guys over the next morning, they got me out of the hotel and over to his house. When you start a cycle like that, you've got to finish it. Bill went away for that weekend then and there I was in the house and there's a bottle of Scotch in there, like stuff and its bad. I mean it drinks. I stayed drunk for a week there.

And I finally went back to Albany and back to the Ford Motor Company. I showed up there Monday morning. And uh, the superintendent met me at the clock and said "Where you been." I said, I've been down in New York. I was taken sick ptomaine poison, yeah? (Audience Laughter) "That's my story, and I'm going to stick to it." Get going back to work. I met a man back there, straw boss, didn't like me. Sour apples and I guess the feeling was mutual. I want to work on the machine. I was an inspector in the springs division and I picked up a leaf of a spring and was putting on the testing machine. So he said, "What are you doing back here. We got a crane broken down out there in the yard. We've got to unload steel by hand; now get out there!" And out I went, into the yard and unloaded with this other guy. And I swear by the end of the day my hands. I couldn't open them, they were just cramped with that flat steel. Bale after bale, bundle after bundle. I used to drive back, back and forth to Albany, with a man, and we shared expenses, and we got in the car after the day. He said, "I tried to raise some money for you. I know damn well you need a drink. I said "Never mind raising the money. I got it, let's the nearest saloon. Well that's the last I ever saw of the Ford plant. That was it. A couple days later, a few days later the man appeared from the Ford Plant one of the security men, and he had a check for one days pay, and he asked for my badge.

So from then on I was right back in the same old situation again drinking; staying sober for a few months, getting drunk again no incentive to live. I knew I was doing wrong. I knew that, I knew the answers, but I couldn't apply them. And this went on as a very unsatisfactory situation. I spent a couple of summers in Kent, Connecticut at High Watch Farm which was the first alcoholic farm, health farm, in this country. I helped run that I was assistant manager. And then, when the man who ran that went on to Beech Hill in New Hampshire in Dublin New Hampshire I went out there with him. I was there In (19)46 and (19)47 I was out in Connecticut, and (19)49 I was in Beech Hill in New Hampshire and I helped him run that, and I was sober as long as I had responsibilities, and something to do and when that ended I went right back the bottle.

And I checked around New York and kicked around New York. I spent some time at a place called the Chester Crest. That's a ... they call it the New York home for intemperate men. It's now gone out of existence. It's too bad because it's quite a place, and they worked you pretty hard out there on the farm, doing work around the place and they gave you five meetings a night. You had to attend five meetings a night and twice on Sunday. And believe me; I got my fill of meetings and then did the same thing right back again. So that brings us up to the summer of 1953.

And I was there in New York. And when I come from this place up there, I'd gotten drunk and got kicked out of there. And I was wandering around New York. I used to drop in the Intergroup which was then at 28th Street and Lexington Avenue. And I must admit I was looking for a handout; trying to get enough to get a few drinks so I got in a place and I get a few drinks, cadge a few more.

And Hazel Rice (Then NYC AA Intergroup Secretary), bless her, came over to me and she said, "You know, I think I got something for you.

Charlie Milton has been over in Paris, France and he ran into one of your friends from the Oxford Group who came to see you originally." And then in passing here I must say that these men deserve as much credit as I do.

For taking the message to Bill, because they brought the message to me. And she said she rang around and that he wants to see you. So she got on the telephone called Charlie and Charlie said, Hold him there till 5:00 o'clock and I'll be down. Well, I waited and 5:00 o'clock Charlie came down. He Said, Where do you drink? And I said, "Over on 3rd Avenue and 28 St. (He Said,) "Come on, let's go over" We sat down and walked to the bar and got a couple drinks; I got a drink he got Coke.

And he said, "How would you like to go to Texas?" Texas, my God who wants to go to Texas? They got no water down there. The cattle are dying all over the place. I don't want to go to Texas; I'm broke. I haven't got a cent to my name and I have enough trouble. He said, "I think it would be good idea to get you out of New York and I think I can arrange that, taking you down there. Maybe some of those guys taking you in on the ranch; get you full of health again." So he bought me another drink and said, "Here's Five Dollars now. You think this thing over."

He said, "I realize it's quite a proposition to swallow all on one night. So I, went home and drank up to my limit, saved a dollar, I take another day till I learned to drink somewhat because of the safety I had gotten so sick of being out in the cold weather out in New York all night long and riding the subways and getting pinched and spending ten days in Rikers Island which is not pleasant.

And it's not pleasant to walk around the streets in the slush all night long, right? I used to walk from 14th Street straight up to 76th and back then over to 42nd Street 5th Ave and down to 14th over again back up. And it takes 3 or 4 trips like that to make a night. Until something opens at 4:00 o'clock in the morning, or if you haven't got a cent. And I guess I learned to hang onto that 75 cents or maybe a quarter; to get a start in the morning. 75 cents to get a bed.

So he repeated the performance he came down at 5:00 o'clock and took me over there, and bought me couple of drinks and then gave the five dollars again. It was a crazy night. I mean he said, "If you want to pick this thing up you come to see me." He says, "Here is where I live and my telephone number."

Well, I had saved enough for the night before that I could go through Friday night and I went through Friday night and then on Saturday morning. I said, "This Is it and I walked up there to see him I went into his apartment house and he was out on the street. I just caught sight of him as he came in. He said, "Well, are you ready to go to Texas?" I said "I don't know about Texas but I quit drinking as of now, last night." He said,

"Let's go up to my room" and we had a cup of coffee and talked it over.

So he told me the Texas idea and he took me out and got me a clean shirt, gave me a hot shower and threw away my underclothes got some fresh stuff and he called Dallas, and got a hold of Ollie Lancaster, Searcy Whaley. As they made arrangements I can hear Searcy or I think it was Ollie booming voice saying, "Alright, sent the Yankee son of a bitch down here." (Audience Laughter) Man, it came Sunday and we got flight reservations for Sunday night, and they put me on that plane. And, I swear, that plane never left circling LaGuardia field, went round, round, seemed to me. I was in a complete fog. And Charlie had a pint of whiskey there and wouldn't give it to me. I told him a couple of years I'm going back and start the whole thing all over again. I want that pint.

Well, they put me up, Searcy Whaley was running the Texas Clinic then at that time and they put me up there, but they didn't give me a drink and they did give me some goofballs and those things just make me nuttier than seven fruitcakes. And the next morning there were a bunch of people, in and out of my room, you'd think I was Exhibit A. They wanted to come in and see this Damn Yankee Curiosity, who couldn't sober himself up, but had been able to sober Bill Wilson up. And there I was going through this thing and if there is anything I don't want is people around me when I'm coming off a hangover. I just want to crawl off in a corner, and there were more people in and out of that room you'd think some Hollywood celebrities being over here. So I just burrowed further under the bed clothes and hid myself and it was fine in there and I turned off the air conditioner. And Searcy came in and said, "Why are you turning that thing off for?" and I said, "Because it's playing music?" And it was, symphony and bands and everything else. I went out on the street once to try to find the band and I couldn't find it.

And I used to stand and look out of a little portal on the front door like one of these out of the way doors. Parking lot and a barracks across the way and I'd see a chair and I'd pull it over and get down over here. I thought that I was never coming back. I mean, it's sincerely. I thought my mind it never... And there was an old colored woman. She said, "You leave Mr. Ebby alone and let him come out of this his own way. They were just about ready to send me to the State Hospital, commit me; because I was gone. I went out walking one night and I don't know where I walked. I walked till 4:00 o'clock in the morning and the Police picked me up. And they put me in one cell after another. I don't know like any developments, they thought I was the leader of a car theft gang because I was leaning up against the car. I had got so tired I couldn't walk any further.

Also, Dickie Sheridan who was another one of my great friends down there he heard about it and he came and got me out. And then I began to shake that off and get back into condition. And recently I began to have some fun around here and I began to go to the A.A. club. I know I walked by it; I'd walk by the darn thing but I was scared to go up the steps. Shaking on the shame; finally, I did I went around and got in the spirit of thing and I began to get some of this Texas spirit which is, you know, it's very great.

And every time I think of maybe I could get the world with a tail again. And I sold some stock in an insurance company which is kind of fizzled, and I got into oil deal which also turned up. With the consequences that after thirteen months I got discouraged myself. I said, I guess I never was meant to come down here to Texas. I should have died there in New York, because I don't think I would have survived another winter. Then I got drunk again.

Well, I didn't stay drunk that long because the law go hold of me, and arrested me, but I got bailed out by guy that was in there that shot himself. But I knew in Dallas. And I was bailed out, but I was back in the County that night for nine days after the half a day in the in the city jail. And when I got out of the County at the end of nine days, one day for good behavior, I was promptly picked up and put back in the city jail. So my drinking was stretched out over about three weeks, but there's only about four or five days of active participation with the bottle.

For them that I had that long period of going right back into that mental depression again and thinking that there was no use, scared to go out in the street, scared meaning that any time I see anybody with a uniform on I turn right around run. I'm scared of that but I got out of that. And began to pick up and then I think finally, I began to realize that things were not going to go well drinking. That I had to accept that and I had kicked myself around which was wholly my fault and it didn't make any difference. The result was there and I kicked myself around so long and it's going to be extremely hard to get a job and then I would have to settle for what I can do, and I went to work for one of the boys there who owned a printing plant I worked for him a year. For the magnificent sum of $37 a week, I think. I didn't have a car, then I was out of work for a while, and I worked with Dickie Sheridan out on the road he's a construction man. I was just flag man on two or three jobs over in Irving around there. And then I worked with Ben Thompson over in the brickyard using reclaiming old brick and stuff selling them for antique brick. And then my present boss came along and gave me this job and I've been there ever since.

And I've been thankful, that I can again assume responsibility and I have been helping out another person in Dallas. And that is giving me some incentive to stay sober so they've been able to get together six years. And that alone has helped me. I am trying to forget the big shot stuff although sometimes in the pressure of money is on it gets hard to go along and not complain about the pricks of life. But nevertheless, I say to myself. If I have lived in, if it hadn't have been for Texas I would have died there in New York. And so I am grateful to Charlie Milton and Cebra Graves in Paris, and Charlie, who put the thing in the motion and followed it through. And it cost him money, and it cost him time and effort to send me down in Texas. And I'm grateful to the people in Texas who are patient with me until I snapped out of it, came out of the fog.

When the gang in New York is discussing women there were a few like Hazel Rice that stuck by me, and figured that I had it in me if they could only get me in the right spot. So I must put aside these things that I think I'd like and things that I want, yet it's not good for me, probably. And be grateful.

But I am alive and able to assume the responsibility of a man and hold a job down. And I am also grateful that I'm able to come out and make these talks. I'm grateful to you people for asking me here; those who put up the money to bring me here, and for my two companions today who took me on such a very good trip. And I must say that the hospitality of California is right on a par with that of Texas, and I want to thank you all.

The End

NOTES

83